IMAGES
of America

MARION *and* HUNGRY MOTHER STATE PARK

One of Marion's first motorized fire trucks, this American LaFrance Fire Engine is parked beside the Smyth County Courthouse in downtown Marion.

IMAGES *of America*

MARION *and* HUNGRY MOTHER STATE PARK

Kenneth Wm. Heath

ARCADIA PUBLISHING

ISBN 978-0-7385-1730-8

Published by Arcadia Publishing
Charleston, South Carolina

Printed in the United States of America

Library of Congress Catalog Card Number: 2004110105

For all general information contact Arcadia Publishing at:
Telephone 843-853-2070
Fax 843-853-0044
E-mail sales@arcadiapublishing.com
For customer service and orders:
Toll-Free 1-888-313-2665

Visit us on the Internet at www.arcadiapublishing.com

An early promotional postcard advertises Marion's big Independence Day Celebration, which is still held every year on the Fourth of July.

Contents

ACKNOWLEDGMENTS

I would like to express my appreciation to all those who generously shared their pictures, postcards, mementos, and memories for the publication of this book: Kenny Sturgill, Brenda Gwyn and the Smyth County Historical and Museum Society, Shannon and Clegg Williams, J.C. Testerman, Dr. Henderson Graham, John Stone, Jim Kelly and the staff at Hungry Mother State Park, Evelyn Lawrence, Eugene Thomas, Jerry Breen, Estel Mack, "Cousin Zeke" Leonard, Stella Maloney, Atwood Huff, Billy Hamm and the Marion Volunteer Fire Department, Rosamond McCarty, Mary-Margaret Justice and the Historic Lincoln Theatre, Greear Studio, Dr. Paul Brown, Renie Hoover, Sharon Chase, Don Francis, Ronnie Harrington, J.X. Hice, and "Big Al" Wisconsin. Also, very special thanks to my production assistant, Cheyenne Gillespie, and to Jada Medley, Todd Long, and Chris King for their technical assistance.

And thanks to my wife, Pamela, for her love, her ever-guiding inspiration, and her support in everything I do.

This is an early view of Hungry Mother State Park and the "Shoreline Drive."

INTRODUCTION

If you are one of the thousands who have gone from Virginia to the "Golden West" or elsewhere, listen! This word about Marion and Smyth County is to show you just what this part of the Old Dominion is now emerging from the ruins of the Great War, young, virile, and with boundless opportunity. And, if you are of any state or country and seek a place to make a happy home, let the printed and pictured facts in this booklet induce you to visit Marion, the beautiful little capital of Smyth County, mid the vales and hills of Blue Grass Virginia.
—From a promotional brochure written by W.D. Roberts and W.L. Shafer, *c.* 1915

Even 100 years ago, community leaders were promoting our town! Welcome to Marion, Virginia!

In 1755, when frontiersman Arthur Campbell settled this area in the corner of southwestern Virginia, it was known as simply as "the Royal Oak Survey." Seventy-seven years later, Smyth County was formed from parts of neighboring Wythe and Washington Counties. On May 25, 1832, the newly established Smyth County Court ordered five commissioners to "lay off the Town at the place designated by the Commissioners appointed by an act of the General Assembly of Virginia to fix upon the seat of Justice in this County." And that is just what they did. George W. Davis, Edward Fulton, Henry B. Thompson, Charles E. Harrison, and James F. Pendleton established the town boundaries within William Humes's wheat and rye fields. The town began at what is now Broad Street and extended westward to College Street. Main Street was 70 feet wide, and Church Street, the main cross street, was set at 50 feet wide, as was what is now Sheffey Street. The north and south boundaries were one block off Main, now Town and Court Streets. The streets and alleys created a "public square," where the first courthouse would be built two years later.

The name was changed on March 15, 1849, as the town was officially incorporated, to honor Revolutionary War hero Gen. Francis Marion, "the Swamp Fox." The town's location was selected for its potential growth. Located on the Middle Fork of the Holston River and along the "Old Stage Road," Marion soon began reaping the benefits of the natural agriculture and lumber resources.

The railroad came to Marion in 1856, and eventually two separate lines traversed the town: the Marion–Rye Valley Railroad reached southward across Currin Valley, and the Norfolk and Southern Railroad roughly followed the Holston River from east to west.

Manufacturing has long been a vital part of Marion's economy. In 1834, Zachariah Shugart built the first saw and grist mill in town. Shortly after, the Humeses built a mill that was later converted into Look & Lincoln's plow, wagon, furniture, and handle factory.

Tourism has also played a part in Marion's history. The first hotel, the Continental, was built in 1835 on the corner of Main and Church Streets. Nearly a century later, the Lincoln Hotel opened across the street as "the only fireproof hotel between Roanoke and Knoxville." In 1936, Hungry Mother State Park opened, located just a few miles from town, and attracted visitors to its sandy beach, cool mountain lake, rustic cabins, and campsites.

Throughout the years, Marion has had her share of interesting people and events. Stoneman's Raid, a two-day skirmish during the Civil War, was fought here in 1864.

In 1895, Snow Flake Flour, a brand made by Marionites D.D. Hull and W.S. Staley, won the gold medal at that year's Jamestown Exposition. Author Sherwood Anderson moved to Marion in 1927, purchased and published the two local newspapers, and is buried in Marion's Roundhill Cemetery. Annie Jones, born in Marion in 1865, had a full beard and moustache by the age of 12, and eventually became the "bearded lady" with Barnum & Bailey's circus. Jerry Freeman, another Marion native, won a contest to name one of America's most famous bus lines with his entry, "Greyhound." Also, the soft drink Mountain Dew was invented here by Bill Jones, who sold his recipe to Pepsi-Cola in the early 1960s for just under $1 million.

Today, Marion continues to be a wonderful place to live. A certified Virginia Main Street community, downtown Marion is being revitalized and preserved for the future. The "center of retail, entertainment, and commerce of Smyth County" sports a unique blend of architectural styles in the buildings lining Main Street in the Historic Downtown District, including the newly re-opened Lincoln Theatre, a 500-seat performing arts center. Hungry Mother State Park was recently recognized as one of "America's Best Parks" and draws more than 180,000 visitors each year.

This town of Marion, situated as it is in the very heart of one of the most lovely stretches of country this correspondent has ever seen—a fair town in a fair valley with softly rounded hills about it and full of good people.
—Sherwood Anderson, *Hello Towns!*

The Armistice Day Parade marches up Main Street, c. 1940.

One

"The Rialto"

Sherwood Anderson, who lived in Marion from 1927 until his death in 1941, said that the entertainment along Main Street was far more interesting and exciting than anything at the movies. His nickname for the downtown area was "the Rialto." This view is from Hospital Hill during the winter of 1947.

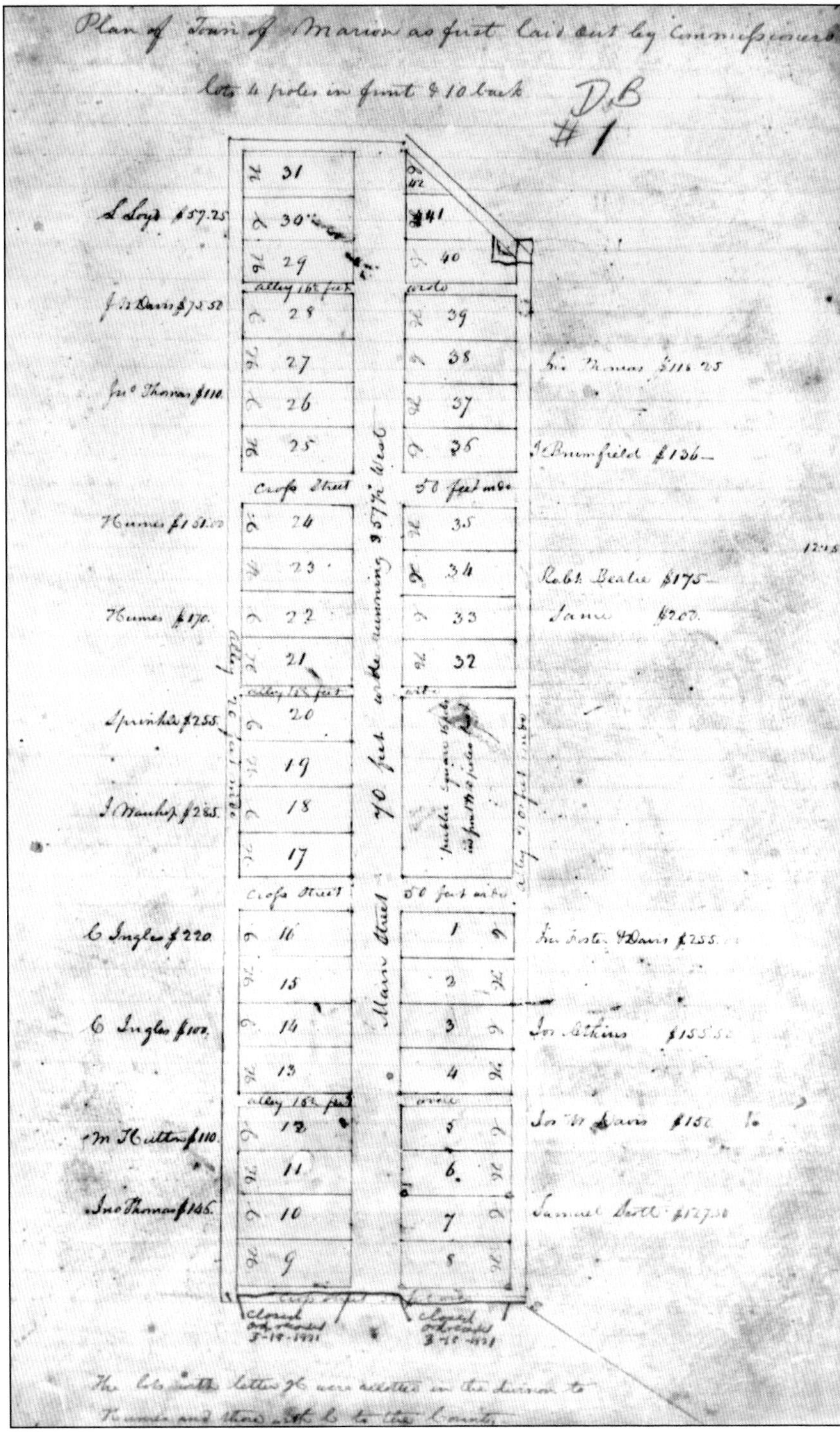

The original plot for the town of Marion was divided into 31 parcels, each measuring "10 poles by 4 poles," or about 165 feet deep by 65 feet wide. The town originally reached from what is now the bottom of Main Street at the intersection of Pendleton Street upward to the intersection of College Street.

This undated photo of downtown Marion was taken from East Main Street, what would later be called "Hospital Hill" because of the construction of Southwestern State Lunatic Asylum. Prominent along the top of the photograph are the spires of the Methodist church on the left and the Baptist church on the right. Most of downtown was still residential, with only a handful of commercial storefront buildings lining Main Street. The streets were still dirt and gravel, and at the intersection exiting Pendleton Street is a horse and wagon.

The same perspective of downtown is shown in this c. 1950 photo. Most of the buildings are commercial, including the ESSO station in the left foreground and the Kroger grocery store midstreet on the right. There are no markings on the street and only one traffic signal, which is located on Broad Street for the Marion–Rye Valley Railroad crossing.

This postcard, published for Roses 5, 10, and 25¢ stores by C.T. American Art, is one of the most famous views of downtown Marion. Looking down Main from the Church Street intersection, this view shows cars parked at an angle, the Lincoln Hotel on the left, the Hotel Marion on the right, and the famous acorn-topped light poles that decorated the streetscape until the 1960s. The small black rectangle in the center of the street was actually a rubber "stop sign," an early traffic control device. The original concrete light poles and acorn globes were donated to Emory & Henry College, and they still illuminate the campus.

This *c.* 1800s photo, taken at the corner of Main and Park Streets, shows a downtown parade. On the left is Sprinkle Hotel, and on the right is the office of *The Democrat* newspaper.

This early 20th-century postcard of Main Street looks up toward the courthouse.

This photo, *c.* 1925, shows the Main Street block across from the courthouse. On the back of the card, the businesses are listed: "Coming up on the right, the Bank of Marion, Jesse Hughes, Leonard's, Sprinkle Drug Store, Post Office, and then the Anderson Building."

In this view of a 1912 parade, the brick Francis building (later Baldwin's) is visible on the left. This building underwent a facade facelift in 1927. The buildings on the right were demolished and replaced with the Royal Oak Apartments and the Lincoln Theater in the late 1920's.

Prior to the construction of the Smyth County Courthouse, courts were held in one room of a log home built in 1766 on the 740-acre "Royal Oak Survey" owned by David Campbell. In 1832, the courts moved to the John Thomas home on Stagecoach Road. Finally, two years later, this building was completed, and the courts had their first official home.

The current Smyth County Courthouse was completed in 1905.

This postcard shows the Smyth County Courthouse. The iron fence has since been removed, and the cannons were donated to be melted down for the war effort during World War II.

This is an early photograph of the Smyth County Courthouse decorated with patriotic bunting.

In this view from the courthouse lawn are the Confederate Memorial statue and the Marion Baptist Church. While perhaps not a major battle in the Civil War, the engagement between the Union troops commanded by Gen. George Stoneman and a much-smaller contingent of Confederates under the command of John C. Breckinridge was important to Marion. The Union troops trying to destroy the nearby salt works in Saltville were held off for two days, December 17 and 18, 1864, by a vastly outnumbered, outgunned Confederate guard. During the battle, nine-year-old Susan Allen got water from the river to extinguish a fire set to a covered bridge by Union troops. They set fire to the bridge two more times, only to have it extinguished again and again by Allen. The town of Marion is featured on the Virginia Civil War Trails program, and a marker commemorating this engagement lies on the west end of town.

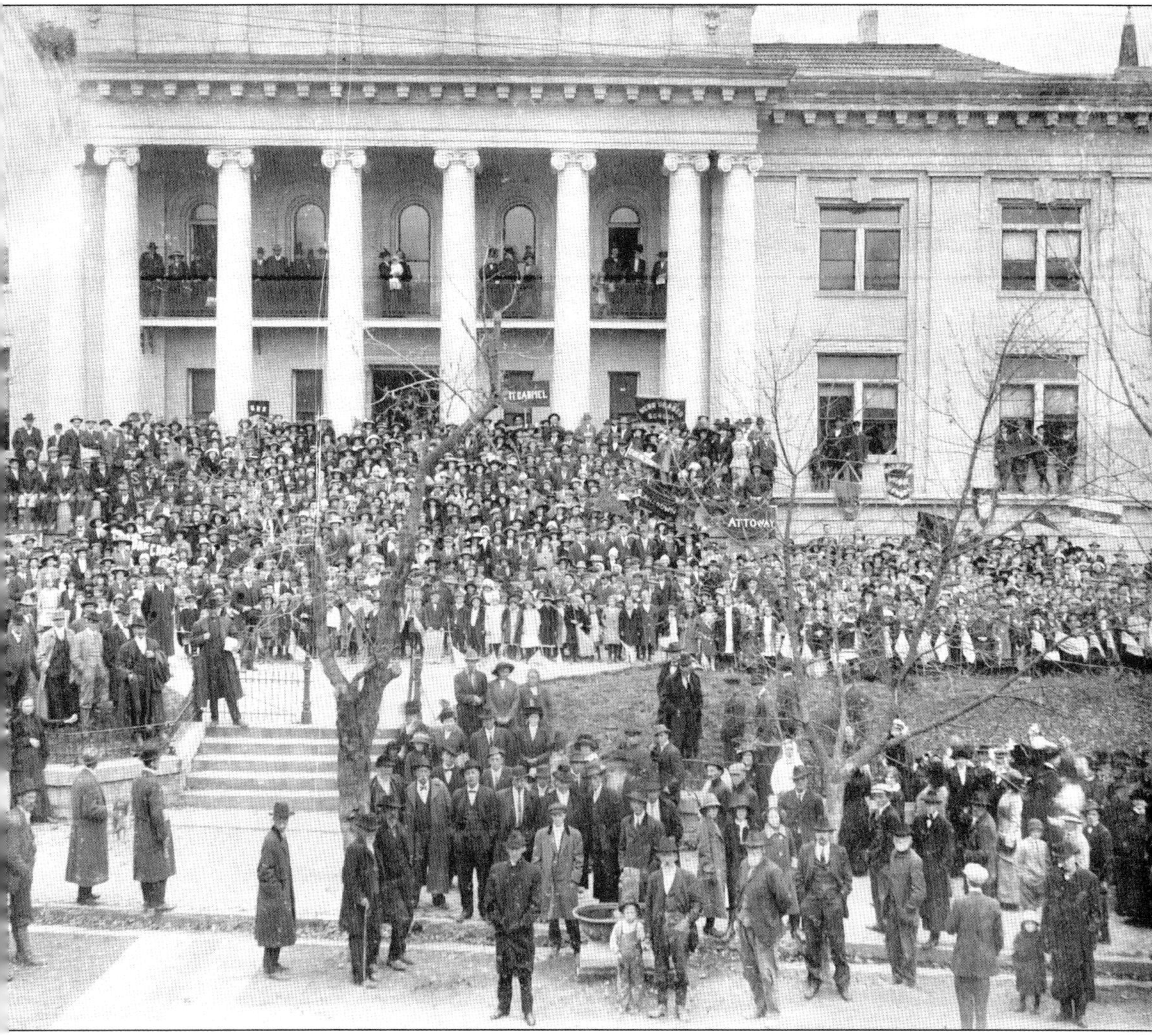

This photograph taken November 1913 depicts the Smyth County School Fair. Students and teachers from every town and school district were represented, including Oak Grove, Mount Carmel, Nebo Graded School, Attoway, Landdown, Ebenezer, and Marion High.

The Jackson Building was constructed by Robert A. Davis in 1850 on lot #32, and J.W. Fell and Minter Jackson purchased the building later the same year for $4,000. Jackson started the Bank of Marion in the first annex in 1874. Four years later, the building became the Exchange Hotel, and in 1913, it was the publishing office of *The American* newspaper.

The first Bank of Marion building was completed in 1897. The structure sat on the current site, and in 1921, the façade was reconstructed, the building was extended another floor, an elevator was installed, and additional professional offices and retail shops were opened. It is still used as the headquarters of the Bank of Marion.

This 1920s postcard shows the Bank of Marion building at the corner of Main and Church Streets; the building is still the headquarters of the multi-state operation. The first year's assets were just over $800, and in 2004, the bank's assets were over $350 million.

The back of this photo of Young's Livery Stable on Pendleton Street reads, "The old 'hack' wagon shown was much used by 'drummers,' or traveling salesmen, to reach country merchants. The salesmen had trunks full of samples for display of whatever was their line of goods."

Shown here is a postcard for the Valley House, an early "traveler's hotel" in downtown Marion.

The Marion National Bank was located at the corner of Main and the Iron Street Mall. The sandstone windowsills along Iron Street Alley on the left side of the building are well worn. As women shopped, generations of men stood in the alley and used those sills to sharpen their pocketknives.

The Hotel Marion is located on the corner of Main and Church, across from the Bank of Marion. It was originally built in 1832 and was later known as the Liberty Hotel and, even later, as the Continental Hotel. In 1910, new owner E.K. Coyner renovated and enlarged the building and added a brick façade. The three-story building had a coffee shop, 80 guest rooms, a pool hall, and a barber shop, and it featured Marion's only revolving door. Behind the hotel on Church Street is the Marion Theater, one of four theaters that were located downtown. The buildings were demolished in 1971 to build the First National Bank on that site.

This is the interior of the City Drug Store, which was owned by Dr. O.C. Sprinkle, Dr. J. Thompson, and Reed Counts. The inscription on the back on the photo indicates that pictured are Branard Williams, clerk; Dr. J. Thompson, owner; and Williams, clerk.

The Goodyear Store on Main Street, advertised as your "easy pay tire store," also specialized in radio repair and sold paint and home appliances. The Marion Chamber of Commerce was located upstairs in the left office of the adjoining building.

This 1924 postcard features Greer's Restaurant and Tea Room, located across from the Lincoln Theatre. The façade of the building has been restored to the unusual Swiss-Tudor style.

This is the interior view of Greer's Restaurant, later known as Wyatt Café. The arches at the rear of the dining room reflect those on the façade.

This postcard advertises the Hotel Lincoln. Named after one of its builders, local industrialist C.C. Lincoln, the hotel was the "most complete hotel in beautiful Southwest Virginia." The detail on the back reads, "the Lincoln is a delightful hotel situated in the heart of beautiful and scenic Southwestern Virginia—on the Lee Highway—US Route 11—the most interesting and direct route North and South. Within fifteen minutes of Marion, over the Parkway Scenic Drive, is the recently created Hungry Mother State park with its beautiful lake covering several hundred acres. When completed, the park will offer every facility for public recreation found in similar parks in other states."

This is a program cover from the grand opening of the Lincoln Hotel. Note the original name was the Francis Marion Hotel. When the Hotel Marion, located across the street, re-opened in 1928, there was much confusion between the two, and the name was quickly changed. Today, the flag medallions are carved "FM" from the original name of the hotel. The original design had a drug store, coffee shop, barber shop, and beauty salon on the first floor; a magnificent walnut-paneled ballroom, tiled cardroom, and bar on the second; and 57 guest rooms on floors three through five.

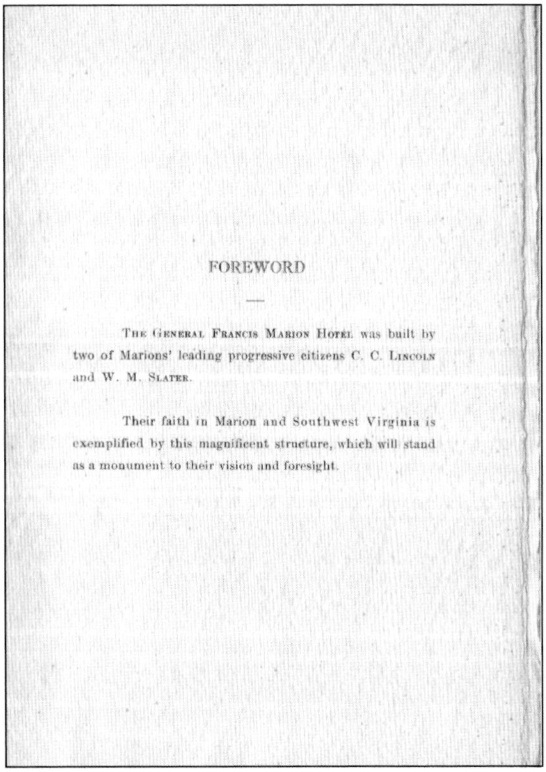

FOREWORD

THE GENERAL FRANCIS MARION HOTEL was built by two of Marions' leading progressive citizens C. C. LINCOLN and W. M. SLATER.

Their faith in Marion and Southwest Virginia is exemplified by this magnificent structure, which will stand as a monument to their vision and foresight.

Here is the foreword from the grand opening program.

This shows the inside of the Lincoln Hotel grand opening program. In attendance were Lt. Gov. B.F. Buchanan and Sherwood Anderson. C.C. Lincoln's wife played the piano for the festivities.

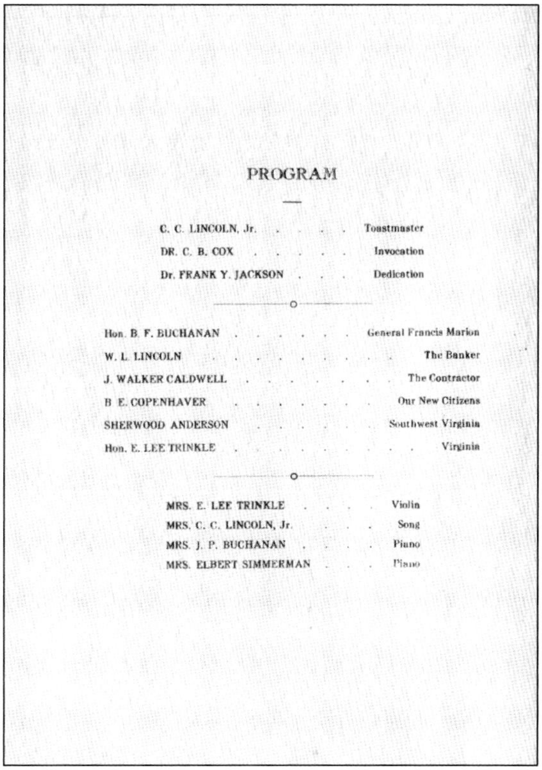

PROGRAM

C. C. LINCOLN, Jr.	Toastmaster
DR. C. B. COX	Invocation
Dr. FRANK Y. JACKSON	Dedication

Hon. B. F. BUCHANAN	General Francis Marion
W. L. LINCOLN	The Banker
J. WALKER CALDWELL	The Contractor
B. E. COPENHAVER	Our New Citizens
SHERWOOD ANDERSON	Southwest Virginia
Hon. E. LEE TRINKLE	Virginia

MRS. E. LEE TRINKLE	Violin
MRS. C. C. LINCOLN, Jr.	Song
MRS. J. P. BUCHANAN	Piano
MRS. ELBERT SIMMERMAN	Piano

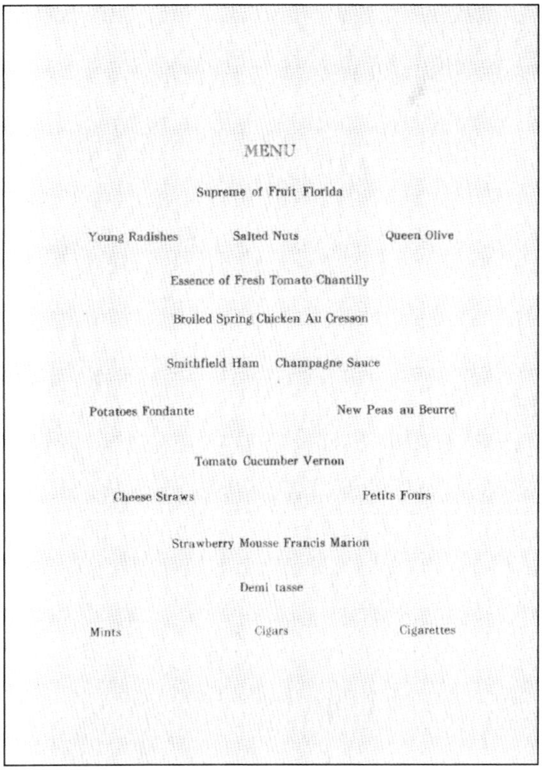

MENU

Supreme of Fruit Florida

Young Radishes   Salted Nuts   Queen Olive

Essence of Fresh Tomato Chantilly

Broiled Spring Chicken Au Cresson

Smithfield Ham   Champagne Sauce

Potatoes Fondante   New Peas au Beurre

Tomato Cucumber Vernon

Cheese Straws   Petits Fours

Strawberry Mousse Francis Marion

Demi tasse

Mints   Cigars   Cigarettes

In keeping with a local Virginia theme, the menu for the grand opening included Smithfield ham and a special dessert, "Strawberry Mousse Francis Marion."

Here is the Lincoln Hotel dressed with patriotic bunting.

The Lincoln Theatre is one of three Mayan Revival theaters left in America. It was constructed in 1929 by C.C. Lincoln in conjunction with C.S. Wassum's Royal Oak apartments, which wraps the theater on three sides. The marquee sits over the permanent easement through the arcade lobby of the apartment building so that theatergoers can access the auditorium. Local artist Lola Poston painted six historical murals along the Lincoln's walls. Billed as "the finest playhouse between Roanoke and Knoxville," the theater opened on July 1, 1929, playing *Close Harmony* to a standing-room-only crowd. The Lincoln Theatre served as the flagship of a chain of movie houses throughout southwestern Virginia. This photograph was taken in the summer of 1957.

In March 1939, the Lincoln Theatre debuted *Gone with the Wind*, and to commemorate the event, the theatre built a Southern-style portico around the marquee.

The Lincoln Theatre featured Grand Ole Opry stars, newsreels, weekly serials, and the top touring groups of the day, including cowboy stars Gene Autry and Roy Rogers. This 1947 photo shows the lobby decorated for a western-themed show.

Shorty Rogers, long-time projectionist at the Lincoln Theatre, stands at his post.

Eleven years after the Lincoln closed in 1977, a community group purchased the theatre with plans to re-open it, but much damage was already done and the building was in despair. This photo shows the crumbling ceiling and plaster, as well as the damage done to the murals.

In May 2004, after $2.1 million in construction, the historic Lincoln Theatre re-opened, just in time for its 75th anniversary. The theatre has been restored and now serves as a performing arts center. Current plans include purchasing projection equipment to show movies in the near future.

Another option for entertainment in Marion was the Seaver Opera House, located on the corner of Main and Commerce Streets.

The Seaver Opera House was given a new look in 1933 when a brick façade was added. Later, in the 1960s, the building's looks changed again when it was sheathed in aluminum.

This photo from 1912 shows "Miss Edna Brown's Recital at the Courthouse Theatre." Listed on the back of the picture are Pauline Moody, Mayme McCready Snider, Anne Moody-Thomas Cottrell, Anna Authenreith, and Tom Moody.

In this Saturday morning Christmas parade in the 1940s, the wagon advertises country hams from I.H. Huff of Glade Spring. The banner reads, "My hams are as rare as a spotted mule. See me after the parade."

Marion's Graded School is located at the corner of Church and Strother Streets. Marion was the first high school established in Smyth County in 1906. During the first two years, classes were held here. A separate high school had to be built in 1915 because of the population increase. And in 1939, a new high school, now Marion Middle School, was opened with 17 classrooms. The first building, pictured here, has served as the town's library, school board office, and probation office, and is currently being used as the Smyth County Museum. The inscription on the card reads, "This is where I'm going to send my kid and I hope you all will too."

Pictured here is the 1915 junior class at Marion High.

This was the first building on the campus of Marion Junior Women's College, *c.* 1873. The Marion Female College, established by the Lutherans, was housed in this old brick residence, which was built by Madison Crockett not long after the town's founding. On January 24, 1874, the charter of the college was incorporated by an act of the Virginia General Assembly. In 1910, the college was closed temporarily. Townspeople and school trustees raised funds to re-open the college and to replace the building in 1911. A year later, the name was changed to Marion Junior College.

This architectural rendering, prepared by Sprinkle and Carson, shows the proposed renovations to Marion Junior Women's College.

This postcard commemorates the opening of the new Marion Junior Women's College in 1911. Male students were not allowed until 1933, and then they were admitted as local day-only students. When the Lutherans withdrew their recognition of the institution in 1967 due to space and financial constraints at the school, the 94-year tradition was transferred to Roanoke College and the campus was closed. Later that year, it was re-opened by the Brunswick Corporation as the Blue Ridge Job Corps, which offered job training for Appalachian girls.

This undated photo shows the May Day pageant at Marion Junior Women's College.

"Old Joshua" was a steam locomotive from the Marion–Rye Valley Railroad. From 1893 to 1931, the line ran from downtown Marion along Broadway (now Broad Street) across the mountain to Sugar Grove. Dubbed "the Scenic Switchback," the rail was vital in the development of Marion's timber milling industry.

A Sunday afternoon excursion departs from downtown aboard "the Scenic Switchback." The railroad was chartered in 1891 by Dr. J.S. Apperson and George W. Miles to develop mineral resources in Smyth and Grayson Counties. By 1893, the rail reached six miles to Currin Valley, and by 1896, it more than doubled to reach Sugar Grove. The line was sold in 1900; in 1901, Jerome Moltz began buying tracts of timber on Pine Mountain for the U.S. Spruce Pine Lumber Company in Marion. The line was again sold in 1905 to Amsler and Campbell. When their lumber mill closed in 1918, two other lumber companies continued to use the railroad until the late 1930s. Campbell's descendants still live in the majestic, yellow brick family home on the corner of Main and Sheffey in downtown Marion.

The Marion–Rye Valley Railroad is headed southbound on Main and Broadway. Included here are, from left to right, S.W. Kent, George W. Richardson, Walter Scott, R.L. Williams, Bob Davis, W.P. Francis, W.B. Wilmore, R.P. Anderson, Will Seaver, Jim Jones, and Frank Francis.

The old depot of the Marion–Rye Valley Railroad is pictured here. After the line was closed, the clapboard building was used as Marion Sheet Metal Works. Now, a brick building stands in its place on Commerce Street.

This 1893 photograph shows the railroad track where it crosses Main Street at Broadway.

This is the interior of Sayers Store, which was located at the corner of Sayers Street and Park Boulevard. Thomas Kelly Sayers (1869–1935), center, had been a stonemason earlier in his life. His patented block machine created a unique block that was used on many of the buildings pictured in the top photograph on the lower end of Main Street downtown, including the theater, a restaurant, and the retail shop that sat adjacent to the Marion–Rye Valley Rail crossing.

Parks-Belk opened a department store downtown in 1941, and people lined Main Street to go inside.

In the 1940s, the Piggly Wiggly grocery store caught fire, and the townspeople filled the streets. The building was remodeled and was successfully operated until 1983. In 1999, after two decades of vacancy, the building was again remodeled, creating five upstairs apartments and two retail shops at street level. A long-standing fixture of downtown, Mathena's Pawn Shop, is still operated out of the basement.

Downtown merchants have always supported the local community. Here, in a 1946 photograph, the Rexall Drug window is decorated to celebrate the 30th anniversary of Boy Scout Week for Troop #91.

Included in this 1946 photo of Boy Scout Troop #91 are Bill Lemmon, George Miles, Dallas Criner, Bill York, Bob Harrington, Charles Harrington, Cecil Greer, Jake Russell, E.M. Snider, John Thomas, and Alvin York. Bob Garnett was the troop leader.

Pictured here is the D.C. Miller Law Office on the courthouse lawn. Miller, a prominent Marion attorney, practiced law in this building in the late 1800s and was instrumental in securing Marion as the site of Southwestern State Hospital. The office has been restored and relocated to the grounds of the Smyth-Bland Regional Library in downtown Marion.

The Marion Masonic Temple is located at the corner of Church and Town Streets. The lodge operated under the first charter of October 9, 1849, until June 17, 1856, when it disbanded. A new charter was granted in 1859. The first lodge hall was at the corner of Broadway and North Alley. In 1909, this structure was built at the corner of Church and Town Streets, and 90 officers were on the roster at its opening. The cornerstone reads, "Lynn Commandry N9 KT, Erected A.D. 1909 AO 790."

This is a bird's-eye view of downtown Marion, *c.* 1947.

Two

People and Places

This photograph shows a giant crowd awaiting the grand opening of the new Parks Belk on Main Street in 1949.

The U.S. Spruce Pine Lumber Company was one of Marion's earliest industries. When the plant closed in 1918, more than 400 million board feet of lumber had been cut.

These are Spruce Pine workers on the job.

Marion Handle Mills, another early Marion industry, produced wagons and, later, tool handles. It was destroyed by a fire in 1943.

This advertisement touted the Marion Handle Mills, another early Marion industry.

The Look & Lincoln factory is pictured here in late December 1942.

Here is the Look & Lincoln factory after the devastating fire on January 26, 1943.

Members of the Marion Volunteer Fire Department are, from left to right, the following: (front row) B.L. Dickenson, W.S. Johnson, Arthur Dean, Paul McCoy, Mark Malley, Burley Morris, Dick Francisco, Preston Collins, and Jack Minnered; (on truck) George Collins, J.B. Richardson Sr., J.B. Richardson Jr., Charles Burch, Everett Francis, Ernest Snider, Tom Moody, Charles Ryder, Penn Francis, Fred Sprinkle, and Joe Stephenson.

In the 1940s, Marion purchased this "modern" Ford V10 Fire Pumper.

Members of the Marion Volunteer Fire Department fight a major downtown fire in the 1940s.

This April 1940 photograph shows the antique equipment of the Marion Volunteer Fire Department. The hand-drawn hose cart, which was replaced by a fire truck in 1921, is currently on display at the new Marion Fire Department building on Main Street. Pictured, from left to right, are George A. Collins, J.B. Richardson, and Everett Francis.

This photograph of the Marion Volunteer Fire Department was taken in April 1940 behind the basement entrance of Town Hall, which the fire department used as its garage and headquarters for more than 60 years. In 1999, the Town of Marion built a new fire hall just down Main Street.

A Marion fire truck draws water out of a creek in the early 1930s.

In a tradition that continues today, members of the Marion Volunteer Fire Department and their spouses gather for a holiday ham dinner. Seated here from left to right are Joe Francis, Edith White, and Howard White. Opposite them at the table are Don Martin (far right) and Eleanor Martin (second from right).

The members of the Marion Volunteer Fire Department (MVFD) join together to build a house for a needy family. Pictured, from left to right, are (seated) Clay Wolfe, Kenneth K. Snider, Bill Johnson, Stuart Stephenson, Charles Snider, Gene Catron, Howard White, Joe Stephenson, and James Webster; (standing) the Walter Stroupe family, recipients of the house.

MVFD member Charles Snider poses in the 1951 Junior Fire Department truck.

The 1966 Marion Life Saving Crew poses with new boats.

The Marion Life Saving Crew works a scene in October 1966. According to an inscription on the back of the photograph, members who are pictured include, from left to right, "Wilson, Armstrong, Kilby, Murray, R. Jennings, and 'Miss Rogers.' "

One of the more popular entertainment destinations in Marion was the Fireman's Jamboree. Here, in a 1949 picture, "Cousin Zeke" Leonard and "King Edward IV" perform with their band on stage. Pictured, from left to right, are Josh Greer, Jimmy Coe, Zeke Leonard, "Duffy" ?, Cotton Goins, and King Edward IV.

In the early 1950s, Cousin Zeke and Curly King are on stage at the Fireman's Jamboree for the Twin City Jamboree special fund-raiser. The Fireman's Jamboree was one of the most popular nightspots in the region, drawing dancers from across the region, including parts of North Carolina, Tennessee, Kentucky, and West Virginia.

Therl "Cousin Zeke" Leonard (right) joined the U.S. Air Force in 1944 and served as a radio announcer on Armed Forces Radio out of Burma. He returned home to Bristol in 1947 and played on WCYB's "Farm and Fun Time" program. In 1948, Zeke went to work for the brand-new WMEV AM in Marion to help raise money for the fire department. He ended up staying at the station for 33 years. In 1954, he was named "DJ of the Year." Here, Zeke is interviewing Cowboy Copas on WSM during the 1954 Radio Convention in Nashville.

Cousin Zeke Leonard, wife Drema, and "Little Zeke" now live in Roanoke, Virginia. Zeke celebrated his 60th year in radio in 2004, and he still hosts a popular radio show each day on WKBA AM.

Another long time DJ at WMEV, George Mizelle hosted "Open Mic," a community gathering place on the radio from 1950 until his retirement from the station in 1982.

WMEV DJ and "one man band," Estel Mac plays nine instruments and has played with many country stars, including "Little" Jimmy Dickens and Mel Street. He was also a frequent performer on the Fireman's Jamboree.

WMEV Studios, "high atop Radio Hill," overlook Marion. The station is the oldest on the Interstate 81 Corridor between Bristol and Roanoke. The call letters stand for "Wonderful Mountain Empire of Virginia." The AM station went on the air December 12, 1948, and WMEV FM joined it on June 21, 1968. Built by Bob Wolfenden and his wife Stella, the stations continue to serve the community.

WMEV station owner Bob Wolfenden signed an advertising contract with area ESSO dealers in 1948, bringing the first radio broadcast news program to Marion.

Vivian Price, a pianist, was a regular performer on WMEV AM 1010. This photo was taken in Studio A in 1955.

The Sturgills Quartet, pictured here with their pianist *c.* 1951, played every Sunday afternoon on WMEV.

In 1959, WMEV went live on location at the grand opening of Carl Vaught's Park 'n' Shop grocery store.

After Wolfenden's death in 1962, his widow, Stella, remarried and managed the stations until she sold them in 1982. In 1964, Marion Junior High School principal Lewis Clay (left) presented Stella Wolfenden Maloney with an award for her service to the community. In addition to managing the two stations, Maloney served as an active member of the Virginia Association of Broadcasters and president of the association in 1972, and she also served as a member of the Marion Town Council.

C.S. Wassum Sr., owner of Royal Oak Boxwood Farm, maintained his farm here in Marion and an office in New York City. The farm is now located on the east end of Marion at the Marion Plaza Shopping Center. This *c.* 1925 photo shows Wassum being dwarfed by his prize boxwoods.

While working in New York, Wassum caught the attention of John D. Rockefeller, who hired him to plant boxwoods in Washington, D.C., at the Lincoln Memorial. This photograph shows the installation of those boxwoods. Notice its similarity to the picture, sans truck, on the back of every $5 bill.

This postcard of Greystone Manor, C.C. Lincoln's home, shows the building's intricate Tudor detailing. Later, it was used as a restaurant, then demolished in March 1970 to make room for an extension of the Holiday Inn on the east end of town.

This view of Greystone Manor is from the front porch of C.S. Wassum's home on Royal Oak Boxwood Farm.

This building, located at 134 Wilden Street, was used as Marion High School between 1938 and 1961. Its original cost was $186,000. In 1961, it became Marion Junior High, hosting seventh and eighth graders. In 1987, Smyth County adopted a county-wide middle school program, and the building was renamed Marion Middle School.

Marion's depot on the Norfolk and Western line was built in 1904. Rail came to Marion in 1856 with the Virginia and Tennessee Railroad. Cattle pens, stockyards, depots, and lumber yards were opened along the line as fast, reliable transportation opened trade for the mountain communities. Abraham Lincoln called the V&T line "the gut of the Confederacy" because of its ability to carry salt from Saltville and food throughout the Shenandoah Valley. Union soldiers launched several raids on the line, burning every station in southwestern Virginia except the one in Glade Spring. During the height of the fighting in 1865, the line was closed for nearly five months. The lines' locomotives were the first to be powered by coal. In June 1870, the V&T was combined with the Atlantic, Mississippi and Ohio line and, in 1881, was purchased and renamed Norfolk and Western. One hundred years later, N&W merged with Southern and became Norfolk and Southern. The station, used for passenger service until 1970, was also used for a railroad maintenance facility until local architect Bill Huber purchased the building in 1993 and remodeled it as retail and office space.

Joan Crawford came to Marion in October 1968 to celebrate the opening of the new Pepsi-Cola Bottling Plant. A large stockholder in Pepsi, Crawford received equal billing with local radio personality "Cousin Zeke" Leonard in the news reports. Here is Crawford, Zeke, and Bob Jones. Pepsi-Cola became a large part of Marion's economy after it purchased the recipe for the soft drink Mountain Dew from Marion's own William H. "Bill" Jones in the early 1960s, making Marion the official "Hometown of Mountain Dew."

Pictured here at the Pepsi plant are, from left to right, Virginia State Trooper Gerald Breen (in plainclothes), Trooper Roy Sneed (in plainclothes), unidentified (woman in front), Marion policeman Buford "Tooney" Overbay, Joan Crawford, Marion policeman Wiley Colley, and Trooper Breen's infant daughter, Lynn.

One of Marion's largest employers, Brunswick manufactured a variety of products, ranging from billiards tables to bowling pins to items for the defense contractor side of the company. In 1961, Marion mayor Guy B. Denit bowled a strike down what had been named Shugart Drive to celebrate Brunswick's 15th anniversary and to rename the street Brunswick Lane.

As part of the 1961 anniversary celebration, world-class pool shark Willie Mosconi came to Marion to unveil a new Gold Crown series pool table by sinking a few balls on the table and playing a few rounds with factory workers at the plant.

Another of Marion's leading employers is Southwestern State Hospital. The main building was erected in 1887 as the Southwest Lunatic Asylum. The combination of "custodial care and medical assistance" treated such mental instabilities as "bite of spider, religious excitement, and melancholia." The facility included a tubercular wing and a building for the criminally insane. In 1888, records indicated that nearly one-third of the 336 patients recovered. The original superintendent, Dr. Harvey Black, would have enjoyed seeing his philosophy of returning patients to their communities finally gain widespread acceptance in the 1970's, as the hospital's mission changed. Now, Southwestern Virginia Mental Health Institute occupies only a small portion of the original space.

In 1888, members of the hospital staff and their families included John Apperson, Dr. John S. Apperson, Georgia Apperson, Kate Gibboney, Nell Apperson, and superintendent Dr. Harvey Black, who was a former Confederate Army surgeon.

Marion was host to the annual Smyth County Fair, circuses, carnivals, and even horse races. Here, competitors take to the dirt track around Fairground Hill.

The Marion Kiwanis Band was one of Sherwood Anderson's passions. In his 1929 book *Hello Towns!*, a collection of articles and essays from his newspaper, he writes, "One of the first signs of the decay of a town is when it cannot get up enthusiasm to support a band. The Marion band needs support. Most people don't know it. Marion is so used to having a good band that it takes the institution for granted. It has always been a straight band. During the eighteen years of its life it has gone to a good many other towns. No one ever saw one of the boys drunk or misbehaving. In order to keep themselves up to snuff the boys practice twice a week. They pay a dollar a month out of their own pockets. This isn't fair. Who will pay the yearly dues for one band boy?"

Baseball Hall-of-Famer Nolan Ryan pitched his first professional baseball at Marion Stadium. He is pictured in the middle row, fourth player from left, in this 1965 team photo of the Marion Mets.

Local celebrities also helped along good causes. In April 1955, Stanley Byrd, Dr. Henderson Graham, Jim Ritter, Roger Copenhaver, and Frank Atkins performed a variety of pantomime, singing, imitations, and more for a "Womanless Beauty Pageant" to benefit the Marion Band.

This aerial view of White Top Mountain, near Marion, shows the arrival of First Lady Eleanor Roosevelt for the White Top Music and Folklore Festival, organized by Marion's Annabel Morris Buchanan in 1933. More than 20,000 people attended the event. The promotional piece for Huff Flying Service details the action: "In the left hand corner near the top is the cottage where she occupied during her stay at the White Top Music Festival. In the center of the picture the large pavilion can be seen. This picture shows the summit of the mountain, which has an altitude of 5678 feet."

Marion's first "chain" restaurant was Ray's Kingburgers, a regional fast food restaurant. Pictured here in April 1979 are district supervisor John Heath (left) and Marion store manager Wayne Berry counting hamburger wrappers after a successful sales promotion.

One of Marion's "tourist courts," Ward's still operates on the west end of Marion as Lorenzen's Motel.

City View Motel, on the west end of Marion, is now made up of private residences.

The Cedars Motel, just outside of Marion on the Lee Highway, was another popular tourist stopover.

Kids from across the region attended summer camp at the Cedars, a Baptist recreational camp located west of Marion.

The Cedars camp featured a number of barracks-styled cabins, a swimming pool, and an outdoor amphitheater called "the Vespers" where church services were held for the campers.

The back of this 1940s postcard for the Virginia House Restaurant says the establishment is located "one-half mile east of Marion." The building was razed in the early 1970s to make way for a branch office of a local bank.

he Health Center of Zeta Tau Alpha Fraternity is located near Marion, Va., for the benefit of the mountain people of Currin Valley

This postcard features a "mountain clinic" near Marion. The sorority of the Greek letter organization operated the facility for about 20 years, from the 1920s through the 1940s.

In the 1920s and early 1930s, Main Street was much different than today. The very lot where Marion's municipal building now stands was, at the time, a miniature golf course. Seeing the need for a strong building to serve as the home of our local government, Marion leaders purchased the lot from C.C. Lincoln Jr. for $5,000 on November 24, 1934. Construction was completed on the Flemish-bond brick, Colonial Revival–style building, with its two stories and three bays, the next year. On July 5, 1935, Marion Town Council held its first meeting in the new building. In 1935, the original structure cost $25,000 to build. More than 50 years later, Marion remodeled the building, constructing new offices on the basement level and restoring and updating the original entryways and rooms. Spectrum Designs, under the direction of Marion's own Bill Huber, provided architectural and engineering services. An elevator and handicapped access was added, and the council chambers were wired for amplification of sound and for future broadcast of meetings. The cost of the renovations in 1999 was $736,000.

The Marion Post Office, a WPA project, was completed in 1935. Before then, the post office operated out of the Anderson Building at the top of Main Street across from the courthouse.

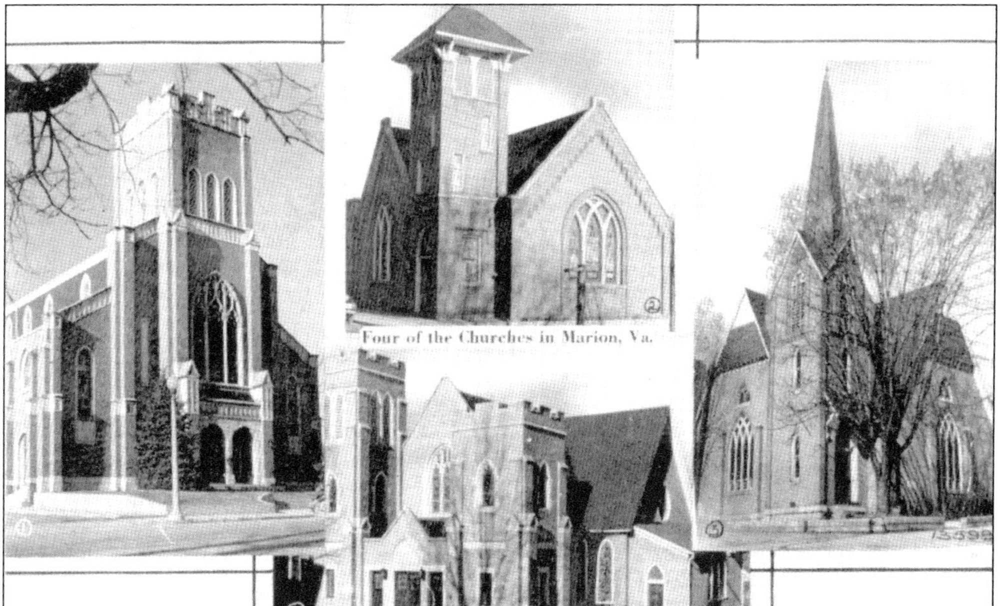

The "Four Churches of Marion: Presbyterian, Lutheran, Baptist, and Methodist," were all located downtown until Marion Baptist moved to the east end of town. Royal Oak Presbyterian Church, after the original name of the town, was the first church in Marion. In 1765, John Campbell purchased the Royal Oak Survey, a tract of land in the center of what is now Smyth County. In 1776, he built a log church on what is now the Royal Oak cemetery, located behind the Marion Baptist Church. In 1880, Ellen Sheffey donated the lot on the corner of Main and Sheffey Streets, where the third building was erected. The current sanctuary replaced the old church in 1923 and was dedicated in April 1924.

This early photograph shows Highway 11 (Lee Highway) leaving Marion on the east side. The first road on the left of the photograph is now Wassona Circle, the second leads to C.S. Wassum's Royal Oak Boxwood Farm, and the road on the right is now Brunswick Lane.

In 1942, Lamb's Gas and Oil was located on the east corner of Main and Staley Streets.

Rosemont, "the Oldest House in Marion," was built in the late 1780s and demolished in 1997. It was the residence of author Sherwood Anderson, who moved to Marion in 1927 and married Eleanor Copenhaver in 1933. He purchased both local newspapers, *The Marion Democrat* and the *Smyth County News*, and published both until he combined them into what is now *The Smyth County News and Messenger*. Anderson also wrote two books here, one particularly on Marion and Smyth County titled *Hello Towns!* He also maintained a mountain retreat he called "Ripshin" in Troutdale. Anderson died in 1941 and is buried in Marion's Roundhill Cemetery. His distinctive sail-shaped marker reads "Life, not Death, is the Great Adventure."

In addition to writing, Anderson was very active in the Marion Kiwanis Band and in the Marion Volunteer Fire Department. Here, Anderson is pictured with the crew in 1941. Pictured, from left to right, are Vivian Wheeler, Robert Lane Anderson (Sherwood's son), Anderson (in glasses), Howard White (wearing a toboggan), Joe Stephenson, and Harry White.

Mack Sturgill, self-proclaimed "Historical Gossip of Smyth County" (1927–1998) was a world traveler, student, author, teacher, avid stamp collector, and local historian. He returned to Marion in 1980 and began his work collecting and writing histories of Smyth County. He served as president of the Smyth County Historical and Museum Society and was active in many other community organizations.

Three

Marion's African-American History

A cast of students of Carnegie High School poses before a performance c. 1940.

This is the Marion chapter of The Household of Ruth, a sister organization to the Fraternal Grand United Order of Odd Fellows, in 1880.

This image shows a joint meeting of the Mount Pleasant Methodist Church groups: the Women's Society of Christian Service and the Methodist Men, in 1952. The church was organized by ex-slaves in 1871. In 1914, the original wood building was replaced by the present brick church under Rev. G.J. Hedrick. The original bell, chandelier, clock, and pump organ are still in the church.

The Charlie Cooley family (pictured here) and the Tom Smith family were brick artisans, laying brick across Virginia. Some of the more notable projects of Cooley and Smith in Marion include Southwestern State Hospital, Carnegie School, and many other churches, banks, hotels, and private homes. Pictured are, from left to right, the following: (front row) Jean, Charlie, Vasser, Rose, and Mary Ellen; (back row) Douglas, Charlie Bruce, and James.

Members of the Smith family pictured, from left to right, are Frank, Tom, Tom Jr., "Jack," and Alphonso.

Many activities revolved around the church. Here, in a picture from the 1940s, is a "womanless wedding" at Mount Pleasant Methodist Church.

Another event at Mount Pleasant, a "Tom Thumb" wedding, features children of the church.

The C.A. Davis Recreation Center operated from 1945 until 1965 next to Carnegie High School. When Hungry Mother State Park denied swimming and other privileges to African Americans, Rev. C. Anderson Davis, pastor of Mount Pleasant Methodist Church, became the founder of a center "to provide wholesome recreation for Smyth County and other neighboring towns' black citizens." The center had a swimming pool, swings, slide, merry-go-round, a shelter with benches, and a four-room cinderblock building with a canteen, men and women's dressing rooms and showers, and a storage room. The cost to swim all day was only 25¢!

Carnegie High School coach George Elliot shouts instructions to his football team. Bennie Woods (foreground) takes a time out.

Pictured is the cast of *Ghosts of Hilo*, a 1946 production by Miss Evelyn Lawrence's Carnegie High School Girls Chorus. On the back of the photo is inscribed: "This musical drama, with charming music, witty dialogue, native Hula rhythms, and an authentic-like backdrop with erupting volcano (red light) was designed by Carnegie student Frank Smith, who later became a professional artist for the U.S. Army." *Ghosts of Hilo* long held the distinction of being the only high school production to be presented on the stage of the Lincoln Theatre.

In this 1950 photo of the Carnegie High School Children's Operetta, Evelyn Lawrence arranges Phyllis Smith's crown in the production of *If I Were a Queen* at curtain time.

Here, the class of 1907 of the Marion Negro Graded School poses with Principal Charles F. Broady. All of the students of the graduating class that year were girls.

Rev. Amos H. Carnegie was the pastor of Mount Carmel Methodist Church and the founder of the only Smyth County high school for African-American students, Carnegie High.

Pictured here are Headmaster R.H. Claytor and the first- through ninth-grade students at the 1919 Marion Negro Graded School. The school was built around 1878 from old, used lumber and was the only school for African Americans until 1931. It was nicknamed "the Old Red Barn" because in 1929, Rev. Amos Carnegie said, "the interior was so dilapidated that it wasn't even fit as a barn for cattle."

In the early 1940s, the Old Red Barn was finally torn down.

Carnegie High School was built free of charge with labor donated by the African-American citizens of Marion and money donated from the local African-American families and their relatives living as far away as New York. The school was adjacent to the C.A. Davis Recreation Center and swimming pool. During its 34-year history (1931–1965), 19 women and 7 men served as faculty in the school.

Susie Madison Thompson, a dedicated pioneer in Smyth County education, was the first African-American teacher in Sugar Grove, and she taught in one-room schoolhouses in Emory and Pearisburg. She is the mother of Evelyn Lawrence.

These are the descendants of Sarah Elizabeth "Sallie" Adams, a slave girl in Marion. In the 1840s, Sallie was sold on the slave block on the old courthouse yard to a local family while her parents were sold to a man from Lynchburg. At Marion's Sesquicentennial Commemoration in 1999, Sallie's granddaughter, Evelyn Lawrence, recounted her story: "To help her with her anguish, Sallie would steal away and put her arms around an oak tree behind her home and cry her eyes out. In 1853, when Sallie turned 12, her owner gave her to his son and moved her across Main Street, away from her beloved tree. Sallie remained with her new family until the end of the Civil War in 1865. She remained in Marion, was twice widowed, and had ten children."

In 1999, the Town of Marion commemorated Sallie's story by dedicating a marker to her and her "Crying Tree" during the town's sesquicentennial.

Four

Hungry Mother State Park

The Dance Pavilion at Lake Forest was the predecessor to Hungry Mother State Park. Three men—E.P. Ellis, Frank Copenhaver, and Dr. J.D. Buchanan—served as directors for Lake Forest, Inc., and in October 1929, began building a recreational facility on Hungry Mother Creek. The facilities included a small lake with a diving platform, bathhouse, picnic areas, a restaurant, and a dance pavilion built over the water. The lake was illuminated so that swimmers could enjoy the water until 9 p.m. When the possibility of a state park being located here arose, the officers deeded their holdings to J.D. Lincoln just three years after Lake Forest opened. The ruins of the pavilion still lie near the middle of Hungry Mother Lake.

Eugene Baker Thomas was a mechanic and truck driver in the Civilian Conservation Corps at Hungry Mother State Park in 1933.

A convoy of corpsmen arrive at the site in August 1933. President Franklin Delano Roosevelt promised the Commonwealth of Virginia enough workmen to build six parks. Companies 1249 and 1252 were the first to arrive.

The Marion CCC Troops are pictured here at morning formation. Eventually, more than 600 men would work on the new park.

Pictured here is an unidentified group of CCC corpsmen.

This is Hungry Mother State Park during construction in the winter of 1933. The unusually harsh winter was particularly tough on the CCC corpsmen because they were still living in tents. Barracks would not be constructed until later.

The CCC troops initially erected tents up Lewis Branch at Tipton Bottom. Approximately 130 men from three units set up camp. Company 1259 located in the valley near the dam site. Companies 1252 and 1249 located here at Tipton Bottom, on the upper end of Mitchell Valley, in October 1933.

Later, the troops built more substantial housing on the sites. Each camp had five barracks, a mess hall, a bathhouse, and officers' quarters. Recreation buildings were added later on. Each camp had its own water system and electric plant.

Eugene Thomas poses at his cabin in 1934. The mess hall is pictured in the background.

Two corpsmen pose on a newly constructed log bridge. When not working, the 600 young, unmarried men "caused secret excitement among the female population of Smyth County and, undoubtedly, much apprehension in the minds of their parents," according to local historian Mack H. Sturgill.

In the winter of 1934, Eugene Thomas stands in the park by Hunger's Mother Creek, which was the creek's original name. On January 10, 1934, CCC corpsmen from Company 1259 put on a vaudeville show at the Lincoln Theatre. Company 1249 did the same the following week, and Company 1252 entertained a week later. Singing, dancing, comedy skits, and tap dancing made fun fare for the Marion community.

Hungry Mother Lake consists of more than 108 acres of mountain-cooled water. Situated on Route 16 between Walker Mountain and Little Brushy Mountain, only six miles from downtown Marion, the park was originally named Forest Lake State Park.

CCC corpsmen excavate near the spillway.

The corpsmen head back to camp after a long day's work. In addition to building the park, corpsmen were put into service as firefighters in the spring of 1941. A 5,000-acre forest fire ravaged Iron Mountain, and the men of the CCC worked for weeks to extinguish the blaze, one of the largest ever in Smyth County history.

Pictured here is the spillway at Hungry Mother. By damming up the creek, a 108-acre lake was created, which allowed for fishing, swimming, and boating. The last company at Hungry Mother, Company 2388, left camp on Monday, June 30, 1941. A small detachment stayed a bit longer to pack and ship equipment. The camp buildings were given to the Marion Chamber of Commerce. Eventually, all of the buildings were razed.

An unidentified young CCC corpsman poses on a log bridge.

Four corpsmen pose in front of the cabins at the CCC camp in 1934.

Unidentified CCC corpsmen pose at Hungry Mother camp. Many corpsmen of the CCC, nicknamed "Roosevelt's Tree Army," joined the military when the CCC was discontinued in 1942.

Corpsmen clear a trail to Molly's Knob at the new park.

Local leaders J.D Lincoln and C.C. Lincoln began building their vision in October 1929, when they sold a parcel of property for $16,000 and purchased the lake property. They donated the land to the State Corporation Commission to build "a recreation and amusement park." Over 1,500 people visited the park during its first Sunday of operation, and for many years, Hungry Mother was the most visited state park in Virginia. Mr. and Mrs. Gardiner S. Plumley of Charleston, West Virginia, accompanied by Nell Preston of Seven Mile Ford, were the first regular customers, and Jack Simmons and Alvin Palmer were the first official swimmers in the new lake. Swimming cost 15¢ for adults and 10¢ for children. "Swim cards," allowing a dozen swims, were available for $1 for children and $1.50 for adults. Lifeguard Maynard Harlow offered free swimming lessons. Tom Cox ran his LaSalle sedan between Marion and the park beginning on July 17, 1936, charging 24¢ for adults and 15¢ for children for a round-trip fare. The car was replaced with a bus the following year, and the route expanded to Sugar Grove.

This is an aerial view of opening day at Hungry Mother State Park, 1936. This was the first of the six new state parks to open that year, and officials from across Virginia were on hand for the dedication of the new Virginia State Park System. This photograph was taken by Dave Greear as Oliver Huff piloted the plane. Virginia was the first state to develop a planned system of parks. Each location was selected to be within 50 miles of "every community of any size." Hungry Mother is located at the southwest corner of the plan. Other parks included Fairy Stone, Staunton River, Douthat, Westmoreland, and Seashore.

This postcard of a "Water Pageant" showcases the bathing beauties on the opening day of the park.

Hungry Mother quickly became the most visited state park in Virginia and only later fell second to Seashore State Park at Virginia Beach. In this vintage postcard, swimmers and sunbathers enjoy the cool mountain water and warm sunshine.

This is a view of Hungry Mother Park Lake Drive and the custodian's home.

This card is "An Unusual View of the Lake and Bath House in Foreground." The bathhouse was quickly outgrown. On July 12, 1936, over 600 swimmers crowded onto the beach. This prompted a plea from Robert Anderson in his *Smyth County News* for an expansion: "Already a scant month after opening, some of the facilities in the park are badly in need of expansion."

One of the more popular postcards from the series of Hungry Mother Lake shows sunners on the sandy beach.

The sandy beach at Hungry Mother is directly attributed to John D. Lincoln, a prominent Marion leader. The state commission refused to provide the sand, so Lincoln rented boxcars and sent it to Virginia Beach. The boxcars came back to Marion with over 1,500 tons of sand, which was trucked to the park and spread over the beach area. The commission then approved beaches at all the other state parks to be covered with sand.

On the back of this "Lake Scene" photo postcard from the 1940s, it says, "A look down on the 108-acre lake at Hungry Mother State Park, near Marion, Virginia, one of the six state parks operated by the Virginia Conservation Commission, Richmond. Hungry Mother Park has cabins and a guest lodge for rent and trails leading to scenic mountain points."

This is a "Lake and Beach" photo postcard. In his book *Hungry Mother: History and Legends*, historian Mack H. Sturgill states the reasons he believes account for the popularity and success of Hungry Mother State Park: "It was the only park in the system connected with a main highway by its own parkway, it was said to be the most beautiful of all state parks, and it certainly had the most unusual name."

One of the best photo postcards shows the sand-covered beach at Hungry Mother Lake. One cliché often repeated about the park was, "Hungry Mother Park is prettier than its name!"

Even those who don't swim can enjoy the scenic drive along Highway 16 North, a Virginia Scenic Byway.

One of the early names considered for the park was simply "Southwest Virginia State Park," as evidenced by this late 1930s postcard with a spectacular view of the surrounding mountains. "Hungry Mother" is based upon an old legend that sprung from the original name of the creek flowing through the park, Hunger's Mother. There was much discussion over the name. Many people called it "deplorable" and "dreadful," including the widow of Lt. Gov. B.F. Buchanan. "Walker Park" (after the nearby mountain) and "Royal Oak State Park" (after Marion's original name) were other choices offered for the name, but the lure of the tragic tale seemed too great to pass over.

In addition to several cabins, Hungry Mother State Park has a rustic guest lodge and restaurant. This is an early view of the restaurant. The Restaurant at Hungry Mother still operates, offering delicious food with a view.

This is one of the original log cabins at Hungry Mother.

Shown here is Hungry Mother's main gathering place, Hemlock Haven. The facility, complete with dining hall, is near several lodge cabins and "The Pines" recreation field.

Hemlock Haven has since been remodeled into a conference center, hosting groups large and small from across the southeastern United States.

This postcard photograph shows the lake's famous high dive in use.

This is a postcard view of "Bathing Beach and Hungry Mother Park." From August 13 to 15, 1937, government photographers came to Marion to include Hungry Mother State Park in a motion picture to publicize the parks. They included shots of people swimming, sunbathing, picnicking, playing mountain music, and even dancing downtown at Wyatt Café.

The inscription on the back of this postcard reads, "The Park covers 2139 acres, boasts a 108-acre freshwater mountain lake, and is Southwestern Virginia's Favorite Playground!"

Pictured here are "Dogwoods in Bloom at Hungry Mother State Park." At one time, all of Park Boulevard leading from Marion to the park was lined with dogwoods, but unfortunately, a blight destroyed most of the trees. Recently, a local group of volunteers, "Friends of Hungry Mother," has begun replanting hearty varieties of dogwood along the drive.

Pictured here is "Cabin #5" from a postcard series dedicated to the cabins at Hungry Mother State Park.

The beach at the lake is full in this image. Lifeguards used a rowboat to get from the beach to the high dive. Rowboats and paddle boats are also available for rent.

On the back of this postcard of Hungry Mother Park, it reads, "Having a good time, August 7, 1940."

This 1940s view shows early boaters in their canoes. In the 1950s, the park added two-person paddleboats and, in 2004, kayaks.

This is an early postcard view from one of the surrounding hilltops. On the back of this card, the lake was called simply "Big Lake at Hungry Mother State Park."

View of Bathing Beach and Lake, Hungry Mother State Park, near Marion, Va.

In 1937, all seven cabins at Hungry Mother State Park were constantly full, and reservations had to be refused. At the same time, at Douthat State Park in Clifton Forge, only about half of the 32 cabins there were rented. Hungry Mother continues to be a top destination today, with cabins and campsites booked sometimes a year in advance.

Looking over Bath House to Bathing Beach, Hungry Mother Lake, Marion, Virginia

The bath house provides restroom, shower, and changing facilities, in addition to food and drink concessions for beachgoers. This postcard looks over the bathhouse onto the sandy beach.

This is the postcard view from the concessionaire's home. The original design of the park by architect C.B. Kearfott featured a sweeping divided boulevard from Marion to the park.

A gravel road leads from the main campground area to the guest lodge, overlooking the back side of the lake.

This photo shows the island, now connected to the mainland by a bridge. Its amphitheater hosts music every weekend during the open season.

This is one of the quaint cottages near Hemlock Haven. The postcard details the amenities: "Hungry Mother State Park, near Marion, Virginia. Facilities include bathing, swimming, fishing, boating, picnicking, restaurant service, hiking on mountain trails, with a lodge for overnight visitors, and cabins for more extended stays."

Here are two cabins near the lake at Hungry Mother.

The name Hungry Mother State Park was officially used for the first time on October 16, 1933. At the very first announcement of the park in Richmond on September 11, 1933, it was called Forest Lake State Park. It was also called State Recreational Area #3 for a short time because it was the third site that had been donated to the state to be used as a park.

The Hungry Mother Grill and Store is now the Restaurant at Hungry Mother and Gift Shop.

HOW HUNGRY MOTHER PARK GOT ITS NAME

The story goes that a raiding party of Shawnee Indians crossed the mountains and desolated several settlements on New River. Among the persons killed was the husband of Molly Marley, and, following the custom of the tribe, the woman and her baby were carried off by the raiding party to their base. In some way the woman managed to escape with her small child.

Eventually, after feeding on berries for many days, she collapsed at the foot of what is now known as Molly's Knob. The child, unable to rouse its mother, wandered down the creek until he reached a group of houses, and, being quite young, could say only the words, "Hungry — Mother — Hungry — Mother." The creek was named Hungry Mother Creek and the park took its name from the creek, which runs through it.

GREEAR STUDIO
CAMERA AND GIFT SHOP
"Center of the Center Building"
MARION, VIRGINIA

FILM - FILM FINISHING - CAMERAS - GIFTS - HAND WEAVING

This flier explains the legend behind the name "Hungry Mother": "The story goes that a raiding party of Shawnee Indians crossed the mountains and desolated several settlements on New River. Among the persons killed was the husband of Molly Marley, and, following the custom of the tribe, the woman and her baby were carried off by the raiding party to their base. In some way the woman managed to escape with her small child. Eventually, after feeding on berries for many days, she collapsed at the foot of what is now known as Molly's Knob. The child, unable to rouse its mother, wandered down the creek until he reached a group of houses, and, being quite young, could only say the words, 'Hungry—Mother—Hungry—Mother.' The creek was named Hungry Mother Creek and the park took its name from the creek, which runs through it."

BIBLIOGRAPHY

Anderson, Sherwood. *Hello Towns!* New York: Horace Liveright, 1929.

The Smyth County Heritage Book Committee and Don Mills, Inc. *Heritage of Smyth County Virginia 1832–1997*. Marceline, MO: Walsworth, 1997.

Sturgill, Mack H. *Hungry Mother: History and Legends*. 2nd ed. Marion: Tucker Printing, 2001.

Wilson, Goodridge. *Smyth County History and Traditions. Published in Connection with the Centennial Celebration of Smyth County, Virginia 1932*. Reprint. Radford, VA: Frank I. Detweiler, Commonwealth Press, Inc., 1976.

One story has it that Sherwood Anderson, his son Robert Lane Anderson, and a handful of co-conspirators decided that the original park name, Forest Lake, was not catchy enough. Since the younger Anderson owned *The Smyth County News*, he published "the Legend." The story became well-known, and the name was changed, giving Marion the state park with the most unique name!